SONGS OF BLOODY HARLAN

By

LEE PENNINGTON

Illustrated by Jill Baker

Winchester Cottage Print

Louisville, Kentucky 40243

SONGS OF BLOODY HARLAN

By Lee Pennington

Published by Winchester Cottage Print

In Louisville, KY

Printed by LSI, Nashville, TN

U.S.A.

Cover and Book Design by Jill Baker

Illustrated by Jill Baker

Second Edition

Printed in the United State of America

ACKNOWLEDGEMENTS

The author wishes to acknowledge and to thank the following publications in which some of these poems first appeared:

The Angels

Approaches

Tomorrow's People

Poets' Theatre

Scenes from a Southern Road

Merlin's Magic

The Guild Anthology

Prairie Poet

Poet (India)

Cyclo-Flame

Lyrismos

The Guild

California Writer

Prism International

North American Mentor Magazine

Original Cover Design by Jill Baker

DEDICATION

For my former Harlan County
Students whose names and lives
Will forever be a part of me

SONGS OF BLOODY HARLAN

CONTENTS

ILLUSTRATIONS by Jill Baker

FOREWORD TO FIRST HARDBACK EDITION OF SONGS OF BLOODY HARLAN

By Jill Withrow Baker

Lee Pennington was born to tell stories, with stories being the main source of entertainment up and down the hills and hollers of Eastern Kentucky. It was no wonder, that, with his gift of writing and of empathetic connections he became a teacher of writing, a dramatist and a traveling poet, reading his poetry in as many as 50 places per year.

Along the way, he has held myriad jobs in order to support his habits of smoking good pipes, telling good stories and eating good food. He became a folk singer, a movie consultant, a protest poet and a teaching consultant to many schools for the writing of poetry. Today, having given up pipe smoking, he has also become a film-maker, a popular speaker and a historian, as well as still being a writer of poetry, writing poems almost daily.

Over his long tenure, Pennington has been lauded and awarded for his poetry. He was awarded the honor of being Poet Laureate of Kentucky early on and won numerous awards for his poetry and for being a successful teacher of poetry for almost 50 years. Three of his books of poetry have been nominated for the Pulitzer Prize.

The late Jim Wayne Miller, a poet who taught at Western Kentucky University, analyzed Pennington's technical skill.

> Pennington's artistry is in his integration of form and subject matter. Just as he can take an old form and make it new and at the same time an appropriate vehicle for his subject, he takes man's experiences of woman in every time and place and renders them with vividness, immediacy and particularity. (*Mountain Review*, Summer 1978)

His words have had an impact upon American society. Once, as editor of the student newspaper at Berea College, he wrote an editorial about integration after African-born soccer players were not allowed on the field of a Southern Baptist college. The editorial was eventually read at the annual Southern Baptist Convention during a motion to integrate their colleges. The motion to integrate all their colleges was rejected, but Carson Newman College integrated their campus because of it.

In the 1960's, after graduation from Berea, Pennington went to Harlan County to teach poetry to Kentucky Community College students. Under his tutelage, they published four books of poetry, *Spirit Hollow, Thirteen, The Long Way Home and Tomorrow's People.* It was this last book that got him in trouble, as the students were honest and frank about their locale, religion and relationships, and local authorities took offense. So much so that a price was put on Pennington's head and he had to leave with armed guards to protect him. This, of course, made national news and he was asked to speak all over the United States.

It was not the students or the population of Harlan County who hated Pennington, but the establishment, the executives, the law-enforcers and managers who disapproved of his freedom and honesty. As Jean W. Ross writes in the *DLB Yearbook,* "the students' work was in part critical of strip-mining, traditional religious teaching, and the hypocrisy of authority." She writes of Lee's subsequent book on the subject,

> *Songs of Bloody Harlan,*, published first in *North American Mentor* (Summer 1971), and in book form in 1975, is Pennington's toughly realistic but ultimately loving tribute to the region that had driven him out in 1967. He wrote of the poetry's genesis, "For two years following my experience in Harlan County, I didn't say anything. But a poet doesn't have that choice either. . . . *Songs of Bloody Harlan* is my comment." (Jean W. Ross, *Dictionary of Literary Biography Yearbook 1982*, p. 335)

Pennington's book, *Songs of Bloody Harlan* was one of his early publications, with a small edition of 100 printed, in 1975. Its popularity grew until it became very valuable, with a high price of $2,500 listed for one available on Amazon in 2018.

Pennington has published more than 10,000 articles in hundreds of newspapers, such as the *New York Times, Louisville Courier Journal, Huntington Herald Dispatch,* and the *Greenup News.*

He has over 1300 published poems in over 300 magazines and anthologies in America and abroad: *Cyclotron, American Bard, Experiment, Trace, American Weave, Alaska Review, California Writer, Seydell Quarterly, Ole, Scrivner Magazine, Caravel, Poet India, South & West, North American Mentor, The Fiddlehead, Arena, Prism International, Red Clay Reader, Southern Poetry Review, Playgirl, Laurel Review, Kansas Quarterly, Poetry Dial, Kaurri, Poetry Venture, Wisconsin Poetry Magazine, Jefferson Review, Wind,* and on and on.

He has published fifty plus short stories in a variety of magazines: *Bluegrass Woman, Laurel Review, Snowy Egret, Hoosier Challenger, Mountain Life and Work, Appalachian Review, Mountain Review, The Hearthstone,* etc.

His 21 published books are listed herein, along with his nine dramas. Pennington is a prolific writer, with yet another book coming out later this year. His long-term relationship with me, his illustrator, began with this book, *Songs of Bloody Harlan,* when I was asked by his editor if I would illustrate the cover, over 40 years ago. I had illustrated other books of poetry, including Frank Steele's *Walking to the Waterfall.* Lee saw Jim Wayne Miller's book, *The More Things Change the More They Stay the Same,* my illustrations in it, and asked his editor if I could illustrate his forthcoming book, *Songs of Bloody Harlan.*

Imagination is the medium of the art Lee works in. I have illustrated dozens of Lee's books, poems and articles. In illustrating Pennington's poetry, I respect his wild imagery, his way with words. I strive to capture this imagery visually. In an article written about Pennington teaching Paducah children poetry at the McNabb Elementary School, in *The Paducah Sun*, (January 5, 1984) Celia Brewer praises Pennington's ability to engage every child's imagination immediately, saying "Imagination, after all, is a poet's stock in trade."

Pennington lives in the real world, but in the world of imagination as well, sensitive to its changing seasons, every waft of air, every spring flower or falling snowflake. He lives every minute of his life, breathes every breath of air, feels every sun ray upon him and touches the rain and earth with respect and awe. Living is art, and he tries to express it in words. As he says, "Butterflies live only a few moments, and even that's enough."

NOW PRESENTING LEE PENNINGTON

By John Edward Westburg
Editor of Westburg Associates Publishers, who first published this book

Lee Pennington, American poet and teacher, born in 1939, as he says, "In one of Kentucky's many hollows in a place called White Oak which is located in the western end of Greenup County", was number nine in a family of eleven children. He said, "I took the hoe when I was eight, a plow when I was nine, the 'lead row' when I was eighteen. I attended the same one-room school which my mother and father attended and carved my initials near theirs in the weather-beaten boards. I taught my first class when I was in the fourth grade…" (because the teacher there had the older students teach the younger ones). He said he loved to write themes in high school, his "Toadfrog Tears" then being "good enough to publish" in *Mountain Life and Work.* Another article which he wrote and which was published in the *Portsmouth Times* earned him a $1,400 fellowship in journalism at Baldwin-Wallace College in Ohio. He said "There has never been a happier young man in America than I when I arrived on the campus of Baldwin-Wallace." Later, he and his wife, Joy, entered Graduate School at the University of Iowa in September 1964, where they both earned their M.A. degrees in English.

In the autumn of 1965, he and his wife began teaching at Southeast Community College in Cumberland, Kentucky, where he served as chairman of the English Department.

In the autumn of 1967, Lee and Joy went to Jefferson Community College in Louisville where he initiated "The Jefferson Players" who in their first semester presented 17 plays, helped establish the college newspaper, and organized "The Path of Poets Series" to bring poets to the campus.

Not only has Pennington edited the now famous little 80-page book of poems, *Tomorrow's People,* but he is the author (to this author's last count) of at least three books of poems: *Scenes from a Southern Road* (1969), *Wildflower…. Poems for Joy* (1970) and *April Poems* (1970).

One reviewer, James Goode, said of Pennington's *Wildflower… Poems for Joy*, that it contains "some of the greatest passion and love I have ever read. Comparable, probably, only with the relationship between Elizabeth and Robert Browning." The poems are about the love between two people, Lee and Joy, at a time when they were faced with a crisis.

Bill and Lanelle Greer, editors of the excellent magazine, *Writers Notes and Quotes*, said of Pennington's *Scenes from a Southern Road,* "of all the books of poems which have flowed across our desk in these five years of publishing and editing *WN&Q*, we feel this book to be the only one we would buy for our own use. In our opinion the majority of poems in this little book are superb and deserving of a place alongside the best American poems (or British either, for that matter)." Of the same book, Jesse Stuart said "Poetry flows from him when he is talking to people or teaching students in his college classes. My feeling now is that if Lee Pennington continues to live and write, his creativity will stand and if submerged it will be resurrected in some distant future." And Clair Emerson, editor, *Hoosier Challenger* (Ohio), said "The collection overflows with what Lee's eyes, ears and heart lived in Appalachia. You can almost smell the Land of the countryside, see the people who live there, and feel the hills and Nature envelope you as you read his poetry."

Pennington began writing poetry seriously in 1962, having by the time "a trunk full of poems." In 1963, he had 11 poems published; in 1964, 57; in 1965, 179 and in 1969, his first book of poetry. His best year was 1970, when publishers accepted and published more than 300 of his poems and published two more books of poems.

In 1967, however, he published his first book not of poetry, but of criticism, *The Dark Hills of Jesse Stuart*, a critical study of the novels of Stuart.

By 1971, he did the dialect for Metro-Goldwyn-Mayer's cinema, "The Moonshine War," released that year. Since then he has had three plays produced: *The Porch, The Spirit of Poor Fork,* and *Appalachia, My Sorrow* (this last as a book). As a journalist he had published ten thousand articles by 1971! He is currently a weekly columnist for the *Greenup News*.

Pennington is in much demand as a folksinger. He gives frequent folksong concerts all over America, singing both his own songs and those which he calls "Poetry of the People," which he has picked up throughout the land.

Pennington's excellent reputation as a teacher is equal to that of his work as a poet.

As a teacher, he truly inspires his students. This ability of his has attracted the admiration of newspaper and magazine people who may be, perhaps, more receptive of this kind of talent than even the so-called professional educators are.

In the *Kentucky Kernal* (February 1, 1966), in an article by Bruce Ayers, it was reported, "Since he's (Pennington) arrived at the community college here, he has been an inspirational influence to his students. So far they have had 43 works of creative writing accepted in nine different national magazines. Last semester his students began publishing *Spirit Hollow*, a magazine of short stories and poems. Explaining that his students seem to become excited quickly about their writing, he said, 'I think that the reason might be that these students, having lived in an area branded with poverty and called depressed, are naturally excited to find that their writing is as good as that which comes from any other region. They are realizing they don't have to take second place to anyone, anywhere. I felt and still feel that Harlan County is one of the most interesting places in the world and this is certainly in my opinion conducive to good writing.'"

Ayers further quotes Pennington, "Students need to be given the freedom to write.... We give the so-called great writers such freedoms, yet we deny them to our students."

In 1966 Pennington was acclaimed in Kentucky as "The Young Teacher of the Year", and Jesse Stuart (by then Kentucky Poet Laureate) in the Ashland (KY) *Daily Independent* (newspaper clippings in the writer's possession, undated but published toward the end of May and early June, 1966) did himself and Pennington the honor of writing a series of four articles in tribute to the inspirational teaching and writing abilities of Lee Pennington (the articles were entitled, "Student Promise Fulfilled"), "And who is Lee Pennington?" rhetorically asks Stuart, "If you don't know him now, if you have never heard of him, I believe you will in the future, both as a teacher and as a writer."

"Last year, continues Stuart, "he set himself a personal goal of having 100 poems accepted and published in one year. He had 183 accepted and published. This must be some sort of a record. He doesn't tell his pupils to do it themselves. He tells them they can do it with him. And while some teachers dream of doing this, Lee puts his dreams into action."

In the Huntington (WV) *Herald-Advertiser* (August 6, 1967), staff writer Dave Peyton, who interviewed Pennington in his native Kentucky home county, said in his article, "Poetry Process: Total Awareness," as follows:

> Outside in the hot summer sun of Western Greenup County, KY, a redbird fought a frantic battle with his reflection in a car's hubcap.
>
> Inside the sturdy frame house in Lower White Oak Hollow a young poet and teacher spoke of his art.
>
> "Listen. Stop what you're doing and just listen," he said, "We're going to listen to every sound. We're going to listen to the sounds this house makes and to every sound outside."
>
> "For a brief moment, there was the stillness which comes from listening.

> "I hear the hum of the refrigerator, I hear the wind in the trees. I hear the redbird hitting the hub cap of the car—fighting with his reflection," the poet said.
>
> "This," he said, "is the beginning of the poetry process. It is total awareness to everything around you. It is using every sense you possess to become totally aware of the world."

Peyton then reports Pennington as saying that the writing of poetry is not for a few gifted writers but for those who are willing to get involved. "It means total involvement through total awareness. It means looking at the world through the eyes of a child." He quotes Pennington, saying, "A poet is one who hasn't been thrown out of the Garden of Eden."

But, Pennington admits to Peyton, the going can be rough even in Eden. "This sense of total awareness is going to cause controversy." Peyton quotes him as saying. "But," continues Pennington, "I have become convinced nothing grows and produces unless there is controversy."

Helen McCloy, a staff writer for the *Louisville Courier-Journal, in her article "Jefferson College Poet Brings Students Alive"* (November 2, 1968) reports that "Students at Jefferson Community College, where he (Pennington) is an instructor of English, say he's teaching them to come alive in the way that he does: by being open to experience, questioning it, and in the process perceiving an answer." She then quotes him, "Experience is the poem. . . . The recording of it is only secondary." She then tells us that the more than 100 creative writing students he has taught in the past three years have over 1,100 short stories and poems in print." "He takes no credit for this. Mrs. Ronald McCray, also an English teacher at Jefferson Community College, disagrees. 'Everyone says he's going to write a book, but somehow those who know Lee do.'"

According to McCloy, "Students frankly admit that they are inspired by the gray-green-eyed, red-bearded poet." Then she cites several student testimonials as to Pennington's teaching style. One student, Susan Coombs, said, "He asks question after question and lets you draw your own conclusions."

As anyone knows, who has ever done much teaching, the teaching and learning process can, indeed, be painful. Pennington's career as a teacher is no exception. Like many of our best teachers in America today, Pennington must realize that only the enforcement of our police laws and the protection afforded us by our federal and state constitutions prevents our most exciting teachers from ending up their lives in prisons or even at the gallows. The prototype of Socrates taking the hemlock of Michael Servetus burning at the stake or Christ at the cross could be the fate of many a present day assistant professor (especially if he has no "tenure"), except for the protection which our laws give today (and hopefully for a long time to come yet).

Yet each year in every state of the Union, barring none, there are cases of professors being fired or eased out of their jobs, which is about as far as our laws will permit us to go in getting rid of teachers who teach our students to think, and often without "due process of law."

Now, in a personal letter to the writer Pennington wrote, in a modest understatement, "Much, yes, much has happened since our last contact (in Iowa). One thing, while I was at Southeast Community College in Cumberland, was violent and nearly cost me my life. Yet, I would do it again, I think. I would stand behind my students as I did then. I do not lean toward violence, yet I found myself carrying a gun to class—this to protect my students which I was prepared to do at all costs."

Pennington is referring to the violent reaction that occurred on the part of the "leading citizens" of Harlan County who became irate upon reading a book of poems which his students had published. Five hundred copies of *Tomorrow's People* were printed, all being sold within five days. County officials, including the sheriff, and the richest men in the community, including a banker, a Baptist preacher, and a steel corporation executive, feeling that the sacred toes of the local establishment were being trounced upon by those maverick kids, tried to bring pressure to bear upon the college officials to get Pennington fired from his job.

Fortunately, as it is too rare among college officials, Dr. Ellis Hartford, Dean of the University of Kentucky Community Colleges, publicly declared about this case, "the matter of teaching tenure is not something for the general public to decide upon. As far as I am personally concerned, it's not for any outside group to tell us how to deal with our faculty. And I don't feel that anyone should question whether students have a right to raise questions about the world they live in. They have a sacred privilege, a right, and a responsibility to raise questions." (Reported in *The Kentucky Kernal* from "combined dispatches," an undated newspaper clipping in the writer's possession).

Also, Dr. James Falkenstine, Director of the Cumberland Community, said in *The Lexington Leader* (article by Walter Grant, also an undated newspaper clipping in the writer's possession) that he had not called for Pennington's resignation. He affirmed, instead, "We have academic freedom, Pennington has academic freedom, and the students have academic freedom."

Yet the pressure continued, especially from among an anonymous and zealous group of hotheads. The pressure mounted to the point that numerous serious threats were made upon the life of Pennington and his wife. Finally, when they received a confidential tip from a student who was in position to know, that a man was determined to shoot Pennington down very soon, the Penningtons gave in, and departed from Cumberland.

The episode, so far as Pennington is concerned, is closed. He has run the gauntlet which others have had to endure, too, some more violently, others less. It has not impaired his teaching or his waxing devotion to his students and to his poetry.

Sharon Sherman, writing in the *Louisville Times*, (November 2, 1968), reported on his career after he accepted a new position in Louisville. She reports that "Pennington won't allow his students to be 'suspended above life on the end of a spider web called college.' They write and submit their work for publication. They file rejection slips—or paper a wall with them—and send their writings out again. No one is happier than the teacher when his insistence pays off. 'It's like a dam bursting,' he explained, 'When one of them gets published, you can't stop the others.'"

She then quotes Pennington, in reference to the reactionary episode at Southeastern Community College, who said "We create myths about ourselves and when they're exposed it frightens us." And again, "Those young people looked at their area—and maybe for the first time they knew the truth. They wrote the truth with love, but the power structure understood."

Miss Sherman then reported that "Pennington picked up a thin, soft-backed book and flipped its pages. 'Look at that,' he said with an edge of bitterness in his voice. His fingers rested on the dedication page, underlining the words: To Harlan County. 'How ironic,' he said. 'They created something and they offered their creation. I don't say all of it is the best poetry in the world, but it's real—it's not false, not fake.... How people can be anything but proud of these young men and women I'll never know.... Those kids have just recorded the poems for a national company. Doesn't anyone see what an achievement that is for a group of mountain kids?'"

Waynette Shackelford, in her article, "Life is for Touching," in *The Kentucky School Journal* (November 1971), has written a revealing profile of Pennington and how he teaches. She said "Recently, while speaking before a poetry class he instigated a session on sensitivity to sight. It was brought out that a familiar object could be seen—with just a bit of imagination—to resemble an entirely different object. This new image could then be used as a descriptive phrase in poetry or other writing. Being aware of the way an object appears could be the difference between dead writing and that which is alive."

Miss Shackelford continues the description of Pennington's technique of "sensitivity to sight":

> The object the class studied was a small, light-weight wooden pedestal lectern, which could easily be moved about with one hand. This was in turn lifted, turned upside down, taken apart and placed on a table in odd and unusual positions. The students, calling out at random their findings for all to share, saw objects in each position in which it was placed. A mushroom, a cannon, a cross such as Jesus carried, and a spear were seen, along with a razor. (At that, Pennington turned to those others who shared with him the distinction of possessing a beard, and said with a voice beginning low and rising as it made its way through loosely clenched teeth, "Get that out of here.")

The students had looked beyond the obvious; seeking other objects in that hard wooden piece, they found them. These objects had become, through imagination, symbols for the lectern. (And one a near threat to our teacher's red-tinged beard).

BOOKS BY LEE PENNINGTON

The Dark Hills of Jesse Stuart (criticism), 1967

Scenes from a Southern Road (poetry), 1969

Poems and Prints (poetry), 1969

Wildflower Poems for Joy (poetry), 1970

April Poems (poetry), 1971

Appalachia, My Sorrow (drama), 1971

Songs of Bloody Harlan (First edition, poetry) 1975

Spring of Violets (poetry), 1975

Coalmine (drama), 1976

The Porch (drama), 1976

The Spirit of Poor Fork (drama), 1976

Creative Composition (textbook), 1976

I Knew a Woman (poetry), 1977; reprinted 2018,

Ragweed (drama), 1980

The Janus Collection (poetry/photography), 1982

Foxwind (drama), 1984

Appalachian Quartet (drama), 1984

The Scotian Women (drama), 1984

Thigmotropism (poetry), 1993

Appalachian Newground (poetry), 2016

Daughters of Leda (poetry), 2017

A FOREWORD

THE POET WALKS

From an Introduction to *Tomorrow's People* by Lee Pennington

The poet walks in the sun and the rain, the snow and the wind, and there is in his hands a soul pleading to know the earth.

His hands are anxious, come spring, to touch the early dogwood blooms, to know a death on death when winter falters, and to know a life reaching toward the sky and roots reaching earthward.

The poet walks in moonlight where shadows speak out like all those yesterdays of the forgotten earth.

His ears hear the songs of roaring mountains and dying rivers and lonely men crying in the streets and children screaming in the night and dogs howling on rat-infested trash heaps and a baby's sigh.

The poet walks in darkness with laughter on his face and tears in his eyes.

His eyes search the black world like a blind man picking roses, like a thin ray of light peeking through a crack in the attic and gathering all the dust particles only the sun can know.

The poet walks in time with the constant clicking of clocks, of beating hearts, of swirling planets, of calendar pages being ripped off and fed to the wind.

He can smell spring coming and winter going and the restless summer days of sweaty July leaves begging dew and the yellow pollen assuring life to the weeds.

The poet walks in life but knows the tombstones on the briar loved hills.

He knows the hungry children crying and the old women laughing, the noisy guns singing in the dark woods and the warm silence of longing eyes, the falling rains and the hot suns, the flowers blooming in the kingdom of the dead, the brown weeping goldenrod stems in the December fields. He knows some young boy sitting alone in the alley and the crowded streets and the dirty rivers washing their way back to clean rain.

The poet walks in youth and sings to the earth, the wind and the rain.
He sings to the high mountains where the wounds now stand out in pain.
He sings to the hissing grass and the lonely streets in the moonlight.

He sings to the windows with broken glass and to the rusty rails and rotting crossties.

The poet walks in Harlan County like the last hope whispering to the darkness, like the last love wishing the sun.

Poetry is a record of his walking.

PART ONE
THE ROAD TO HARLAN

THE ROAD TO HARLAN

On the road to Harlan
Night in deep breath,
Dawn awaits our remembering Yesterday's death.

Fallen behind Black Mountain
The clouds hang wet,
Where leaves knew the wind
Which time never met.

HARLAN COUNTY
(Song in E Minor)

They say don't go
To Harlan County.
A coal miner dead
Under winter skies.
They say don't go
To Harlan County.
They say don't go
Where the sun won't rise.

They say don't go
To Harlan County.
Snow is melting.
Rising flood.
They say don't go
To Harlan County.
Harlan County
Bathed in Blood.

But I must go
To Harlan County.
Wheels are rolling
Rolling me by.
I must go
To Harlan County.
Harlan County
Before I die.

THE STARS HAVE COME

The stars have come,
he said
walking mostly over a cane.
Night, too, is here,
replied to self.
The tap, tap, tapping.

Beyond empty sockets
yesterday's eyes
paint what it was.

Smell of wind.
the same wind seeking
features of face.
The same face seeking
features of wind.

Beside the red bricks
another face, buried
in an overworked hand,
raised an upward stare
where street lamps,
scattering light dust,
covered the stars.

The same hand fell
and came again with watch.
The face fell
from where stars
might have been.

Then the ticking.
Then the tapping.

Hearing into time
and staring.
Staring into time
and hearing.

The stars have come
walking mostly over a cane.

JILL BAKER

SOUND IN THE NIGHT

From Stacey Hill tonight
The only sound I hear
Is a giant semi unleashing
Energy, pushing on the road
Toward Big Black.
That sound comes where
Fog has failed this clear
Night. It is diesel strain
Punctuated by clatter over
Poor Fork Bridge. I think
The sound will last forever
Until my years must strain
To hear near silent motor purr.
Then I am left to know
That there is wasted rest
This late (now when no cars run)
At one of Cumberland's two redlights
Still dancing from last night's wind.
Still warm from yesterday's sun.

OLD MAN

Tonight Poor Fork is restless
Like some lonely old man out walking
Off the blues, kidding a stone
Here and there with no big nothing
To lose except maybe last
Week's shine
And next week's shoes.

NIGHT BELONGS TO WALKING

Walking in Cumberland
with night struggling and
no hopes to win,
of victory complete within
the shell clicked closed.

An old man slow on the walk composed
tomorrow's map
and felt a slap
more evenly across his mind,
felt something stand before, behind
his eyes—
then stood trying to realize
what it was he thought,
what it was he caught
then lost
as night tossed
and turned another way.

Must have been night? Or was it day?

CRAZY ANNIE

All those hours on Big Black
Searching for the old one,
Stopping now and then to watch
Dew overweight leaves and fall
Sound into our ears—we listened for her scream.

Often when low sapling branches slapped
Our eyes and left them red in the dark,
A vertigo vision blinked an image
We thought must be Crazy Annie
Standing out there in the moonlight
With white hair falling in front
And back. We waited for the scream
Which was silence.

It was no task to think Annie there
Somewhere hiding in the dark woods of our mind.
If the moon fell right on droopy leaves
And shadows played with the wind,
We could see her move in and out among
Underbrush and all those falling sounds
Fused the larger screams.
She, the aged goddess of the night,
We were satisfied it was she.

During the downward trip by the stones
Out onto the level path home, we stopped
Long after and listened again to the echoes
Of the hallow laughter which we never heard.

NIGHT'S TOWN

The night is wet with town.

Broken moon falls
forever red
through endless dead-end streets.

Through alleys of the young
kissing.

Past the old man green on the cross.

Dogs are angry
with an overturned
empty can.

Cats lick
their hands.

A puddle
catches a red light
like a song
lost in the bowels.

POOR FORK SUN

Perhaps Black Mountain was the creek stop
where the sun hitched a ride on Poor Fork,
then came tumbling with the day frost high
down Cumberland's sleepy eyed face.

There was no sound of rumble, just
thoughts of rusty bucket waves
and sand-heavy tin cans plugging up mud time.
The sun sliding down the skin of Poor Fork

is stranger to this place; just ask the lookers,
or the brokers who sell wind by fireplugs.
Or a few old broken women with brown bags –
Women grinning at trains at the crossing.

RIVER HAIKU

Poor Fork is silent;
farewell fingers point deathward
in ice a poet.

BEGGAR

I am a beggar of things
only a cup of earth
can hold.

I am on these lonely streets
where the universe
chokes on silence.

My mind walks on crutches
and my blindness
bandaged in white darkness.

PALE SILENCE

The silence I fear most is the pale silence
Down by the river where the wind blows
The restless water into waves of cold trance
And suddenly a duck-like milk carton becomes a rose.

It is the green silence against gray mountains.
Long sweeping scars carved into stillness.
Dry suns etched on dust where a million tons
Of coal once danced in all the dampness.

Such as men standing by the red road
Where all their goodbye hands wave
At no one in the dark night, in the cold.
Who cares anyway how empty men behave?

On such a night when ears drown in waiting
And no voice nor song is ever spent,
Perhaps it is the mind's open mouth left gaping
At the final whisper now brought silent.

PART TWO
BLOODY HARLAN

BLOODY HARLAN

I Down at the edge of the world
By the lonely waters of Poor Fork
Time has curled
A knot of souls.
Someone let pride seep out.
Now the dark winds blow
And men shout.

II Where are your young men singing?
Where the young lassies to sigh?
Are your briers still clinging
To the rocks along the sky?

III "Let me tell you, son.
If you're going to live around here,
You'd better get a gun.
More guns in this county than people.
More churches than preachers
And schools than teachers.
More broken men than gravel.
The county is still on the run.
You'd better get a gun."

IV We came down from sleep
Early and stood around
Waiting for water to
Get back its taste.

V The square brick buildings
Waste morning sun
Where old men sit
Dirty around the courthouse.
Where the breathing young
Dance the song of moon

Wishing day were night
The time of another tune.

VI MINE ARE DEAD STREETS.
LONELY HOUSES WITH BROKEN WINDOWS.
BROKEN FAMILIES WITH FATHERLESS
CHILDREN. MINE ARE THE SONS
AND DAUGHTERS OF REACHING HANDS.
EARS FULL OF SOUNDS OF SINGING GUNS.
THE BLACK FACE COAL DIGGERS
WHO SPILLED BLOOD OF THEM AND THEIRS
ON LONELY STREETS BROUGHT DEATHWARD.
MINE ARE BULLETS STILL WEDGED IN
BUILDING SIDES TOO DEEP FOR SNOW.
STILL THEY WALK MY STREETS RED IN MOONLIGHT.
STILL THEY DREAM OF BLACK MOUNTAIN HOMES
WHERE THE WIND IS CLEAR AND BIRDS LIFT FEET
FLYING SOUTHWARD, FLYING TO GET WARM.
STILL THEY DREAM
AND THESE ARE MY DAUGHTERS
AND THESE ARE MY SONS.

VII The tipple is quiet now
Like a cloud dying in the distance.
The patter of feet is a young boy
On the hot sidewalk. Two eyes
Looking like autumn leaves falling.
Pockets are not big enough
To hold his hands. He watches
The wind he cannot see.

SANCTIFIED MOUNTAIN

He came preaching when weather was Wednesday,
When night saw teeth white in the wind
With blue skin bucks hanging to their women –
The no-father God believers came on to lend

Soul sounds that brought the mountain to its skin.
Men pulled their women and heard big guitars –
Got their feet to stomping, got their arms to swinging
And somehow beat down the rolling brimstone fires.

But he wasn't through, not by a long timber.
When August painted caution spots on green poplar lore,
He came back winded and he came back a preaching,
And Sanctified Mountain rolled out once more.

First Daddy Collins, with his gray spirit eyes
And a long white beard a holding up his chin,
Took a step toward the stumps laid for an altar,
Shouted, "Glory God! Glory God! A-men, A-men!"

Then Sally Burden with the moon on her skin
Bellied off a laugh; her eyes got the jumps.
"Whoop-la, Whoop-la!" Arms were a swinging.
She got down and crawled toward the stumps.

The stumps filled up but he kept a preaching.
The moon came and went; the sun did the same.
The brimstone fires fell something awful
When Sanctified Mountain took on its name.

THE GODS OF BLACK MOUNTAIN

(For W.D. Snodgrass who knows that gods still live on Mount Olympus)

The Gods of Black Mountain are in love.
She walks this valley on night's wind.
You can hear the roaring up above
The treeline where all the Gods send
Immortal cries to earth and she
Is dream where Gods and mortals are.
She is mist when clouds are not free,
Left to disappear with Mercury's star.

Only mortals know the chase of Gods –
Only she the licking of wet tongues.
When goldenrods have turned to brown pods
And touch-me-nots prepare exploding guns,
The Gods come for the falling seeds,
Gather to the wind her flowing hair,
Spread her deep among the valley weeds
And leave a beauty for a mortal stare.

The Black-Eyed Gods also know the pain,
Have felt gathering wetness soak them through.
They know the power of the April rain,
The depth of cobwebs caught with morning dew.
She, too, has walked in the early grass,
Felt the life surge into her feet,
Reached the point where no mortals pass,
The place where Black Mountain Gods retreat.

RIVER HEART OF COLD WINDS

Cumberland, I loved the wind which rocked
Your soul and mine on nights when rain
Came tumbling, enchanting your face
With flying fog and sheets of crystal flow.
I loved the night when all the sounds
Brought snow and tried to chill my heart
Beyond the warmth of love, but this power
Was such a little thing I know
And meant nothing to the open earth.
Fires glow and spread such shadows enough
To claim all the cold the night brought
In. And this I know, I know it so:
All the wind and rain and cold and snow
Cannot stop a bleeding river's flow.

THIS TOWN

This town which has a thousand shiny eyes
Bled across the wound of second snow
Is town drawn under winter skies
Shaded with the shadows of dark crow.

Shaded with the greyness of the wing
And wind so strong to turn the dead aside
To hear singing men with no songs to sing
With calloused lips biting back the pride.

SOUND TONIGHT CALLING

Who are you, sound tonight calling?
What madness is your name where
Moonlight finds a river flowing
Down the channel and white rocks stare
Along the bank? Must have been beyond
The scattered field where I shouted high
Into the wind, felt the nightmare splash
Immortalize my cry –
A cry to live a moment, then to die
Forever –
A rock tumbling smaller in the river.

CUMBERLAND

Cumberland sits in the valley
Like a big frog
or like a grey lizard
on a rough bark log.

Coal smoke spins
to Black Mountain level
and paints a
night devil.

But the people,
the young the old,
the broken church steeple
watchers, have sold

their souls on Poor Fork's
water
and poverty becomes Time's eater
and blotter.

RAIN ON CUMBERLAND

Tonight the rain sinks dryness
like silence of lost moan.
Earth is wet, wet
to flood the shallow ground
and puddle is love.

Wind is artist
on atmosphere canvas where
blacks and greys burp crystal
death to death
and life crawls away
on four feet.

GIANT MAN OF HARLAN

Giant Man of Harlan
Tromping through the trees
Raising young whippoorwills
Stirring up a breeze.

The young men all fear you
And your Giant Hand.
Girls have love on their lips
When you walk the land.

How many have seen you?
Have touched your golden hair?
Have heard your voice of thunder?
Have felt your black-eyed stare?

Tonight the roads are lonely,
Lonely as a crowd.
Young men are creeping
Under some dark cloud.

Dreams will go under;
Men will bury gold.
But the Giant Man of Harlan
None can ever hold.

CRY BLACKNESS

down there
in that gnarled
church house
you send your
mingled prayers
toward some stormy sky

tonight you jest

tomorrow in the fields
behind a mule
in blistering sun
you curse
and whip the mule
come back and
testify
and praise the lord
bless his name
and all the holy ghost
amen

you cry
fiery words
that bless the good
and damn the bad

you cry until you die

you burn your knees
in dry soil
and close your eyes
to dogwood spring
you send your mingled prayers
toward the darkened sky

pray your prayers
and testify
and curse your mule
and plow the soil dry
and like a beggar
look for cause to die

© Jill Baker 2019

HARLAN

Harlan, I know your streets are covered
with coal dust and unmarried women
drag their young hunting men
with hot homes to sleep in on cold nights,
with pork and beans and plastic spoons.

Bloody bare feet slowly click off time
like two tiny plumber's tools in
the sidewalk night. Old fat robins
eat seeds and come flying in to plant
them with self-made fertilizer
on the courthouse square

I know the sounds of the L & N and
the Greyhound bus bringing them back
home. I know Cleveland, Dayton, Detroit
faces, all Harlan men who went away and
made good with a $20 a week taxi job.

BIG JOHN 9

Big John 9 left here thirty years ago
With enough moonshine whiskey to turn Detroit
Into a fancy town, and he found work not as dirty
As "them politicians" or the coal "I left behind."
And he says he got rough as hell out there without
The wind blowing foul country smells into his face.
He said time was when you could walk down the streets
And pull your pants down and hump the preacher's wife
While the kids watched and laughed and pointed,
And got tired and made fun of the dirty youngins
Hungry and playing hopscotch on the railroad track.

Big John 9 got a taxi job and threw away his Harmony guitar
So he could sit around at night and watch T.V. like anyone.
He got so city-fied with curtains up and not spitting on
The floor and driving a big Ford around nights it'd make
Your head swim and he up and came home and cried
"I'm a mountain man, by God!" And he stayed with his sister
While his wife got a city man all hot on what a country girl
Could do and the city man put her and Big John 9's little
Girls in a fine home and had two wives sleeping in his bed.

But Big John 9 had his sister and they went around the street
Holding hands and laughing at the wind and finally joined
Church and heard the preacher tell about brotherly love
So much they were singing glory like a bucket of frogs.

Until the sister up and had a brotherly love baby
And Big John 9 cried about his virgin sister and the
Preacher laughed and laughed and said he'd come visit her.

THE NO NAME

Loneliness is the no name for this town,
Here where loneliness begins.
Like calling a mountain spring
A river and forgetting all the bends
In between. Those crowds below know
Only crowds below as pines know only
Forest in shape of larger sum. Birds gather
Fallen twigs, return to build their nests
Back in the dark wood where death and life
And life again sing songs where so many fly.
Not loneliness but merely shells against the wind
Where autumn empties eggs and peels bark to fall and dry.

©Jill Baker. 2019

PART THREE
SONS AND DAUGHTERS

SONS AND DAUGHTERS

Harlan, only your sons and daughters
know the wind
When rains cut dark chills across your face.
Only the young know love when moonlight
Shows spring buds in blooming race.

Only your sons and daughters know songs.
Their voices deep as your black coal scars
Only they know rivers clean as love.
Only they walk in moonlight hunting stars.

YOUNG EYES

I came down to Harlan not knowing
How bare feet sound on the streets.
I came when the wind was blowing
and birds made retreats.

I found the young here curious,
Their eyes sprinkled with fire.
Young whisper flames in newground
Licking thorns from the brier.

Here I will harvest my soul
In Harlan where the young are hurled
That their warm eyes may stare
Into the night of the world.

CHILD IN GOLDENRODS

My child
Do not cry.
Run under those
Tunnels where only children can.
Goldenrods bloom for your curious eyes,
Your searching hands.

My child
That is not sin
Sticking to your tiny fingers
Where you go to fields of goldenrods
To make playthings
Color the wind.

INTERLUDE

The rain.
The fog.
The old man
pouring water
from his felt hat.
The young child
discovering faces
in puddles.

©Jill Baker 2019

YOU, THIRTEEN

You, thirteen, have my eye,
not because of sun or darkness
but of shadows,
those hiding behind trees
and under the river stones.
I have always felt the half
of either measured time
is where the eyes should be.

So to you my eye
shadow children.

First for M.B.
If I could know the mystery
of rooted thoughts
buried in the top soil of your mind,
as they sprinkle the earth
with thick foliage,
I would be with a cultivating hoe
and work each row to leave you weedless
for the sun,
and this you said I have done,
but I tell you, and it's true,
I have only walked on fields where you grew,
I was only a passer by.
You came through like a seed fallen wild,
immune to regular crowning blight
and dry rot, and now the fruit
ripens of its own, it is so,
and pardon me if I watch with pride
while you grow.

For J.S.
It was you, J.S., who taught me how
lines of grass and stone
and rooster violet fights
beside shacks which house our thoughts
could be the shadows
crawled from their hiding.
And maybe, too, it was hands

soiled from grease and oil
(the car still runs, thanks to you)
unafraid to spot a page
with lines half borrowed from a broken engine,
half from ink,
generating poems of rage
to make us think.

For R.D.
Was it not on the streets of Harlan
where they stopped your walking,
you with your father's gun
you gone mad in a night of shadows
where the darker wine runs?
I remember, yes.
How could I forget?
It is still with me yet
like in February, one relives
the first chill of December.
And didn't they throw you
from God's house (they claim it's His)
and leave you there in space –
these many dogs and wolves
who never know the chase?
Few I know like you
who can carve sun made greyness
from the stone,
(and stones have roots)
then further break to dust
to find the stone's inner darkness.

For K.P.
Many are the hours I sit
before your lines watching
grey curling clouds claim
salt water made in pure rain.
I think how each word
falls accurate next to each
like the faded white separates
road halves where they tried to run you down.
Into the town you came with folded eyes
and love so thick they called it hate,
and it is always that way,

and all their screaming
of being cold and not knowing
you start with warm bodies and then cover;
for starting cold, a hundred coats
will just keep the chill in.

For J.G.
Steel legs pump a poem
out of a midnight moon
down Cumberland's tongue tied roads,
you bound to a racing machine
clicking off the miles
beside railroad tracks.
I liked the image
You sprang on us
Saying there were no brakes
In the race you ran to win.
Behind that long black hair
which crowned your face
I knew there was a gentle soul
aware. I've seen others write lines
on many things, but you were the first
humped over a bicycle
streaking a coal soaked wind.

For J.A.
Perhaps I didn't know it all
till miles removed I read
those words you said
under a reporter's pen,
under headlines heavy enough to break
down any ordinary page.
Already I had heard your sonnets
and that was enough to sing
back falling leaves
where trees stood dripping.
And didn't you volunteer to the world
to leave a land of guns
and go where guns were firing?
Didn't you rip your dreams
from the calendar page
singing every new moon of sorrow?

For A.S.
You, fair one, and I call you fair,
knew the talk more than I
for they loaded it on your being
like thick teeth of iron
and you, perhaps, were more aware
than all of us at the sound of dripping rain.
And could I care if they call you dark haired
mistress of a county claimed sane?
Could I measure motion of a million thought
feathers tickling their gutted brains?
Could I clock the speed of screams
hurled like mental snowballs at your soul?
Is it less to know the ticking
than all the time captured in a stone?
A rock, a stone that used to be the sea,
it matters, yes, as shadowed wind frees
your sound down among the tombs
blowing graves and bleached bones.
Even now the tall shadows stare
to whisper of your sound everywhere.

For C.H.
If they only knew your magic innocence,
it would not have been so tragic
the way you roasted poems over dreams,
the way you carried shadows from the dark,
and sprinkled light on trees to cast a shade.
You, young friend, the only one laughing with wet eyes,
laughing then and laughing still.
And you heard voices in Old Cumberland
each begging to be born as sleep wakes
a restless rattle of chill
over the whole earth when night cannot
be contained. Last night you went warm;
today you wake in rain.
You with bones we found on Pine Hill.
You beside a fallen down shack
where children step on glass
and bleeding feet stain snow.
Today I eat your lines of poets
spreading coal dust on the wind,
and this I would have you know.

Keep laughing, wet eyed laughter.
Laugh everywhere you go.

For L.S.
Young Appalachian mother child,
child of tall blond grass,
creator of sons now men,
dreamer of the wind bird's song,
forgive me if I love you while you pass,
love you as I love the earth and stone
and you a part of all of it.
Earth child the poems you sing are free
as wind caressing a river mist,
as fog swaying to hypnotic tunes
when all the months are June
and all the moments warm whispers of time.
And were they afraid to touch your wings,
afraid of some butterfly stain,
afraid to touch a leaf covered with dew?
Did they not know every leaf and wing
was also a part of you?
Did they not hear the flowers cry?
Did they not hear the grass speak of sun?
Did they not hear blond straws break underfoot
in every field you run?

For R.S.
Your grandfather was right.
I did not tell you, but I have been
out on a river night with cool stillness
breaking in my brain like pecking sand
and I have seen the giant men
drink thirsty from a stream.
I have seen their saucer eyes gleam in mist,
burn like bright phantoms in the moon
of a faded scarecrow town.
They were all around
and made the sound of autumn drums.
But that is no matter.
Lesser men than I have seen greater things.
It's just I want you to know
when you spoke trembling into my ear
that I too did see, that I too did hear.

And when you walked the road alone
and dark eyed mysteries stared at you,
I also walked the road alone
and saw the mysteries too.

For L.V.
Does it matter now?
I mean is it anything now with many fallen leaves?
That day we sat and wept together
it all seemed like tons
of stones fell where we stood.
Looking back, would we change it now,
even if we could?
But I remember then the falling stones.
I think often of it and there is dampness
still not near the hot or cold
but in the chill
that runs the length of my myth.
There is the clatter of bones,
And there is high river water cheating stones
of passing wind.
There always will be water;
there always will be wind.
You, young one, know well the sound:
beauty is as beauty gives.
I've heard you sing it all around,
thank you. I heard you sing beauty found.

For J.G.
You brought out poems
like we come from spring, dancing
our feet clean of winter mud.
I never knew one singing more.
I knew not all the nights you went touching trees
till somehow hands were singing too.
It must have been the breath of frost on a window pane
where you scratched your first line
like faces drawn by a child,
and then you wiped them clean
and blew your breath
to make the frost your own.
Every place I look now
I see your finger drawn faces.

I see the childhood of a window
give childhood to the world.
I see the tiny frosty patterns
and icy shadows curled.
Everywhere I look, and
I look at everything
I have heard you sing, poet;
I have heard you sing.

You, Thirteen.
I grow away from you
but then you grow too
and wherever our wood burns
in the pale odor of night
in the cool magnificence of day
I'll stop to say
from time to time
that the circle turns
dark to light
light to dark
that all is shadow
like some dripping soul
sliding down a straw
and now our drops merge
a greater wetness
somewhere around it all.

FOR HENRI

Henrietti Louis Massengill Hopkins, 1947-1966, was a student in the first Writing of Poetry class ever taught in Harlan County, Kentucky. She was youth; her poetry was spirit. She was married on Saturday and died the following Monday.

This noon I stand
as teachers stand
and gaze into
the downstairs room
where motion goes
on like darkness
descending some ridge.

That ringing sound
in my ear quiets
forever a place
in my soul.

A student.
One who stood in this room
Where chairs are empty
now, where the cocola
clock has stopped.

I remember.
She took a pen from the air.
Wrote poems for the wind.
Now they all blow silent.

Dead, they say.

There is no reason.
No logic.
The light is gone.
The dark world
darker.

GLASS IMAGE

(Lines for M.B.)

When they came and told me,
I screamed inwardly, inhaled
thoughts and coughed image
of what must have been.

There alone in that room
alone in aloneness
alone with aloneness
you, too, must have known
that inward scream
caught in the chest
tearing insides apart.

You must have known
watching world crumble
watching cabinet
above sink
and reaching blindly
staring into that glass
seeing the white porcelain
through bottom side
then the smash
and slivers sprinkled
like snow across your face.

Holding the broken image
pointing hopeward
that pointed to dream
of somehow carving that scream
(already the inner wounds)
You must have laid the edge
across your wrist
and felt the red cream
rush out.

TOO SOON NIGHT'S ICE

Robins too soon on spring
Huddle fat on limbs –
Caught too cold to sing
As the cool sun climbs

To noon, then drifts beyond
The trees. Then final darkness
Where night must be fond
Of strange visitors who press

Against each to form balls
Of black sour ice.
When tomorrow's sun fails
These have paid the price.

PART FOUR
HARLAN, BACKWARD GLANCE

HARLAN, BACKWARD GLANCE

Christ! You can sit around all day
talking blood this county claims
and it's no more than shoes full of sand.

I never knew a man
who did not laugh on words
of dogs eating the guts out of that
one left nine bullets dead
on the garbage heap.

Something like holding a June bug
on a string, letting him fly
above your head.
You can hear the hum of it all,
feel the pull,
but that's all.

Every second is a red memory.

HARLAN WHERE I'VE BEEN

Harlan where I've been
your streets are cold like the last
tears your daughters shed
on Poor Fork's waters.

Your icy hands cannot
touch wounds bled forever
in time.

Harlan streets warped
like green boards in the sun,
of footfalls silenced.

Harlan girls pulling
up their dresses for a
Father's eyes
the color of rain.

Harlan mothers
feeling the soft hands
of Ministers

under the covers –
come to see
them ill,

come to touch and heal.

Harlan officials
licking the backends
of each other,
treading water
of people's souls.

Harlan's law
walking the streets
to watch town girls
undress in windows.

Harlan
where hands shake hands
of a proud father whose wife
is his daughter
whose son
is his grandson.

Harlan where rivers
smile coal dust teeth

and trees
giggle by the road.

BROWN ROSES

I just came from Harlan,
Perhaps yesterday or now,
While the pale roses died
Like crowns of thorns in
Waters where death is brown
Flowers floating by my eyes.

I saw a young poet
Weeping by his heart.
I knew him then
And now.

I knew his dreams
Were webs strung
In the sun.
I knew he too
Had come to watch
The brown flowers.

I saw a young poet
Die by his poem
I heard him sing
Of songless songs.

Burning in the wind
And near the brownness
I came to touch
The water's edge
I came to speak
The river's sound,
But heard instead a poet's dream
Fall silent under ground.

TODAY I DIED

Today I died
In a thousand suns I died
And the earth was swept clean of grass.
All the moon moments were green
Time of all we knew.
Children wept and gasses kept falling.
People prayed and roots grew from their knees.
Rivers melted like icicles.
Sunday broke the silence.

Today I died,
In whirling sands I died.
And now the past of long knives
And hammers bleeding.
Coughed up all we knew of man.
Still not knowing his hand's mind.
Still not believing the God child

Urinating in white skulls
Of three eyes – a hole and empty sockets.

Today I died.
It was warm in the rain,
Wet as the red blood,
Cold as children screaming.

The earth spit up the sea.
Stones fell silently from mountains
Till mountains were unmasked land.
In the cold darkness of universe
Someone stood laughing.

NIGHT SCREAM

This morning I woke trembling by the edge
Of a scream and threw my naked body
Into the day, the stillness broken
Like glass made dust out by the wind.
I woke with that red on black sound
Crushing my cocoon senses and crawled
Groping with long white arms
Set against it all like two antennas
Feeling for the final wall: to stop,
To turn another way, to stop again.
I listened for that cry which broke
The strange patterned scream, images
Set back somewhere between the mind
And eyes. I listened with ears wanting
Growing coal, pale in the dew of morning
Glow, but heard only the whisper
Of the loudest cry, and that silence.
In the blue morning of fear, silence.
By the edge of a hopeless scream.

DULCIMER WINDS

Dulcimer winds play tunes of December,
Cold melody warmed to a ballad made
Here tonight where leaves have long since fallen
Where nude black trees now form no shade.

Still these black fingers play the dulcimers
And I can hear the sharp tunes sweeping low.
I can hear the strings harshly played
As darkness blooms tonight where coal winds blow.

©JILL BAKER

RAIN FOR A FALL

Water eyes watch the world (falling moments)
Covered now with brilliant death, colors all
Singing of grey mist breath hissing here
From depth of a million blond pools. Eyes
Slowed the wind today with crystal pain.
Enough to blow in sheet and patterns
Of multicolored wings, yet slow as breath –
Mirror spoken for the dead. The pitter-patter
Eyes watch an earth caught with leaf burden.
But we, a world our own, back a hand
Across the face to know a dryer motion.
Still those eyes.

CLOSED WIND

The wind closed tonight
Like petals of wild roses
When summer is too much sun
And shadows cry.

The earth kept turning
In the eye of universe
And if the wind had not died
We could have stood the silence.

PART FIVE
YOU SAY YOU WANT TO HEAR?

YOU SAY YOU WANT TO HEAR?

You say you want to hear about Harlan County?
Bloody Harlan County, Kentucky,
Lost in Appalachia lost in itself.
You want to hear about lonely coal miners,
poor and without food,
and working for enough script to walk
down to the company store and buy a sack of oatmeal
and it's cornpone and the fat side of a rock
cooked in polluted river water.

You want to hear about loading eighteen or nineteen
tons of coal a day and walking home with twenty-five
cents you can't spend anywhere but back where you were
digging.
You say babies dying in the streets
and young eight or nine children along women
trying to pull up the covers
to keep God away from it all.

You want to hear about miners digging black coal
and black coal digging a miner's soul
and hungry men deciding by God they'd fight
a vein of company
all the way back to Bethlehem or Pittsburgh
or anywhere there's blood.

And they did fight and you can walk feet
on the names of every battle and likely still
see red stains like there's been a Civil War.

And the Unions pulled them up
and left things better;
then the Machines came on

and we're right back in the middle of winter.

But the old power ain't the same
You can't hear the company stores.
You can't hear the script going cheap on the back streets.
for real money any more.
And men buying up that script and selling
It back to the companies and getting rich.

You can't hear that, but you can
still hear power like there's someone
standing around the voting machine
listening to you vote.
Like someone's been running the county schools
for thirty odd years and his big hands
reach out on the state to slap a few wrists here and there.
Like its all tied up with county officials
who tell you where to set your feet on their streets
and how lightly. Like driving people into the ground
like they are stakes and now there's nothing
but the tiny battered top and sticking up above it all.

Then the county officials stand back and the school people
stand back and say there ain't nothing wrong.
It's all pretty. Like that man
living with his wife and daughter and having
children by both of them, that's pretty.
Like the father giving his armless and legless
daughter a child, that's pretty.
Like the man selling his daughter for three hundred dollars,
that's pretty.
Like a whole mountain side covered with windowless
and doorless shacks, that's pretty.
Like getting mad when those damn natives
of that mountain come begging for food, that's pretty.
Like a little nine hole golf course overlooking
hungry children, that's pretty.
Like nineteen people killed in the county in one month,
one left on the garbage pile with nine bullets in him,
that's pretty.
Like twelve year dead happy pappies
getting government checks and cashing them, that's pretty.
Like bulldozers stripping the land,

covering a broken shack of someone
not able to fight back, that's pretty.
Like thirty whiskey stores in a dry county, that's pretty.
Like making raids on local enemies,
breaking their whiskey bottles on the courthouse square
and running a bootleg joint on the side,
that's pretty.
Like saying nothing is wrong,
none of it exists,
it's all a myth,
that's pretty.

Until some Young Person says:
"Wait a minute;
The emperor has no clothes!"

Then another says: "He's right!"
And another.
And they all sit down together
the sons and daughters of Bloody Harlan,
and they look real hard and say:

"Well, let's look at it the way it is."

And suddenly they see what they see
and what they see is no longer pretty.

But what they say is beautiful
for truth no matter how ugly
is always beautiful.

© Jill Baker 2019

PART SIX
JUST BECAUSE I WANT TO SAY IT

JUST BECAUSE I WANT TO SAY IT

There was a time
When I was afraid and stood
With my love who cried broken petals
Because someone said we'd ruined their children.
Taught them evil things, led them wrong.
And we ran away from Appalachia,
Dark haired mistress, down a million Eden roads.
(They hate us and we hate them and best
They're gone and we're gone, and best the
Children left alone, untouched, unkissed
Left weeping in loneliness).
Just because I want to say it,
Not to set it straight, but to give,
As always I want to give, I shall say
It and it is yours.
I love you and your naked bodies
In the shower houses washing away mountain coal.
And fortune tellers, beggars, and women
Of the streets.
I love you all since I can't help it and
Even if I could help it, I still would love you.
I love your dirty faced children of the streets,
Especially those you found looking for love yourself.
Little boys crying by the rivers and little girls
Holding their hands and kissing their feet and licking stones.
I love your old broken down women
Leading blind dogs.
I'll bow down to your drunk and kiss his hand
And watch his shoes for him
While he's off looking
And the Chief of Police who said I was a son of a bitch,
I love him, and his son,

His son who said he'd kill me
Because one of the children made reference to his love.
And his daughter who wrote poems and filled the dresser
Drawers with them and locked them up because she was afraid.
And the pretty blond haired mother whose husband
Jerked her from a car,
Pulled her from her lover and took her back
Home to a house of weeping sons, I love her
And her pure white tingling skin and eyes full of moonlight.
And the dirty Negroes down by the gas station
On coke bottle crates, smoking and drinking and cussing,
I love them all and will sit with them and kiss their faces.
And your beautiful young girls warm all over, so
Warm they need to touch and give their warm selves to
Anyone who's cold. I love their touch,
Their bits of broken
Laughter and the young men who lie in the grass
With them and touch their warmness under trembling
Hands and thumping hearts. I love your young girls
When they laugh or cry. And the woman who stood
In the dime store and said the songs the children
Sang were songs of love and not of hate. I love her
And what she said. And the misplaced school man
Who called it smut and his wife still looking for Adam's rib
And their young son taught to preach of dirty teachers,
I love them too for they are lonely and lonely is easy to love.
And the young girl who cried because someone said buckteeth,
Because someone stepped on her religion like a snail on stone.
I love her and the blackeyed girl the town said violated
The bed of a hundred husbands and those yet unmarried.
And the little hunchback who wrote coal-mine poems
For anybody's ear and kissed my hand because I listened.
I love him and his singing and his town,
Dirty so much the wind won't pass through the rain falls
Slowly. And the brown-eyed preacher
Who searched the streets
For whores to save,
Who preached that songs of sin
Have found their doom in streets of sorry, who ran
Away a young Lord seeking child
Because the church was too holy for such.
I love the preacher, the child, the songs of sin.
And the young man who sang a thousand songs

And wept a thousand cries and stood by the road and waved
At the sky. I love the woman who said we should have
Zipped his pants and painted him white and taken him
From the dirty railroad track where we found him. And
The boys driving around streets in helmets, and songs
Laughing tears they couldn't cry. And the boy
Who read his Bible to find men of God were honest with
Their words, who cried when scorned for being honest with his.
The play-like scholar who hated things he loved, who found
His mother in the eyes of his moon-eyed wife, who searched
For pubic hairs in the refrigerator and threw jelly out
Glass windows, I love them too and the night which brought
them.
And the man who ate a cake with glass, measured church, sent
His wife to the joint for a keg of beer and the child
They kept trying to have. And the student looking
For his manhood under a soft woman and whiskey bottles.
And another listening to his grandfather tell of giants
Around the campfire on coon hunt nights, hating the world
And the no-god who made it.
I love him, his grandfather, his world, and the no-god.
And the father with his daughter
Wet in his arms like pollen soaked with rain, and the limbless
Child they made in the weeping stillborn world.
And the young man with his heart in his hand,
Dying but singing anyway his songs.
And the long-haired boy searching for love and
I told him I loved him and he cried
Down beside the railroad tracks.
And the boy singing sonnets for his mother
And throwing rocks at tin cans.
And the mothers who made their children write
Letters with dirty words because a poet sang.
And the six men waiting in the shadows with their guns
Hoping to cleanse the place with death and blood.
I love your black faces stained with coal
And your houses stained with age and your tears
Smelling of rain. And all the songs you sing and
All you never sing and all you want to sing.
Your dirty court house square.
Your aged superintendent behind his glass covered eyes.
Your funeral man trading well-prepared bodies for land.
Your cardboard shacks filled with babies, hungry here

Because two bodies came together hunting love, I love them.
Just because I want to say it
I say it. I love you – you naked, naked of clothes, naked
Of ideas, women with warm breasts, women, men, children, land.
All naked and before me and just because I want to say it, I say
It and I hope it does not embarrass you when I do.
I love you, I love you.

www.ingramcontent.com/pod-product-compliance
Lightning Source LLC
Chambersburg PA
CBHW050642150426
42813CB00054B/1157